American Government

OFFICE OF THE
PRESIDENT

John Perritano

THE WHITE HOUSE
WASHINGTON

SADDLEBACK
EDUCATIONAL PUBLISHING

AMERICAN GOVERNMENT

Foundations
Office of the President
Congress
Supreme Court
Political Parties

Photo credits: page 1: lev radin / Shutterstock.com; page 7: Alamy.com; page 8/9: Joseph Sohm / Shutterstock.com; page 35: Everett Historical / Shutterstock.com; page 35: catwalker / Shutterstock.com; page 42: Joseph Sohm / Shutterstock.com; page 43: Alamy.com; page 50: Marco Rubino / Shutterstock.com; page 51: Alamy.com; page 54: Anthony Correia / Shutterstock.com; page 55: Alamy.com; page 63: Infinite_Eye / Shutterstock.com ; page 66: Ryan Rodrick Beiler / Shutterstock.com; page 69: Joseph Sohm / Shutterstock.com; page 70/71: a katz / Shutterstock.com; page 72: lev radin / Shutterstock.com; page 76: Joseph Sohm / Shutterstock.com; page 78: Joseph Sohm / Shutterstock.com; page 79: Twin Design / Shutterstock.com; all other images from Shutterstock.com

ISBN-13: 978-1-68021-121-4
ISBN-10: 1-68021-121-8
eBook: 978-1-63078-436-2

Printed in Guangzhou, China
NOR/0116/CA21600021

20 19 18 17 16   1 2 3 4 5

TABLE OF CONTENTS

Introduction

Article II of the United States Constitution. What is it? It spells out the executive branch. The executive branch runs the country. The president is the boss. Article II has four sections. Each describes the **roles** and rules.

A presidential hopeful must be at least 35 years old. A natural-born U.S. citizen. And a resident of the U.S. for 14 years. The framers wrote the Constitution. They wanted a strong leader. It's one of the hardest jobs in the world. To many, the rewards are few. People dislike you. Write mean things about you. Take you to court. They work hard to make sure you are not reelected.

So why do people run for president? There are many reasons. Some care about history. They want to be remembered. This is a big reason. People want to be known. Others think about one cause. Things like the environment. Or campaign **reform**. It may be important enough to run. Many want to have power. It may be the biggest job in the world.

Whatever the reason, the job is hard. There is a lot of worry. The responsibility is great. Every American soldier killed. Every citizen without a job. Every natural disaster. Every big oil spill. These all become the responsibility of the president of the United States.

President Barack Obama's first four-year term was busy. He signed 654 bills into law. And vetoed two. Three more bills were signed by autopen. Autopen is a mechanical signature. The president was on a trip. He allowed the autopen to be used. In the past a White House worker would travel with the bill. Bring it to the president to be signed.

The president held 19 cabinet meetings. He visited 35 countries and 44 states. Some more than once. He flew on Air Force One 836 times. And on Marine One 801 times. The president met with 131 foreign leaders. And he hosted state dinners at the White House. State dinners celebrate our foreign friendships. They are like fancy parties. Six countries were honored. India. Mexico. China. Germany. South Korea. And Great Britain.

President Obama didn't pardon many people. It was the lowest number since President James Garfield. Mr. Obama "takes his Constitutional power to grant clemency very seriously." That's what the president's spokesman said. Only 22 people received presidential pardons. Of course that number doesn't include two pardons. Each year two Thanksgiving turkeys are saved.

A good president does with executive power what Pablo Picasso did with paint. He takes bills into new and slightly discomfiting territory. He puts extra eyes on policies. He moves the mouth of the Supreme Court from where it should be to where it must be.

—Lyndon B. Johnson

Chapter 1
GOING TO WORK

June 26, 2015. The Supreme Court made same-sex marriage legal. Same-sex couples could now marry. It was a big moment.

President Obama went outside the White House. He stepped up to a microphone. Mr. Obama is the country's chief executive. He praised the court's decision.

"All Americans are entitled to equal protection of the law," he said. "All people should be treated equally, regardless of who they are or who they love."

Think About It: *Does the Constitution limit a president's power?*

[TIME TO INSPIRE]

Later that day the president went to a funeral. It was in Charleston, South Carolina. A white gunman had killed nine people in a church. The dead were African American.

The president gave a speech. His chief-executive hat was off. The chief-of-state hat was now on. As chief of state, the president is a symbol of the nation. The chief of state inspires and comforts.

President Obama talked about **race relations**. He talked about faith. And the president talked about what it means to be an American. It was a moving speech. People cheered when he was done.

It was 1961, John F. Kennedy's **inauguration**. He spoke words of inspiration. "Ask not what your country can do for you, ask what you can do for your country," Kennedy said. These famous words still mean something today.

Up and away. Then 73 seconds later, the space shuttle *Challenger* was destroyed. It was 1986. Ronald Reagan was president. He said, "The future doesn't belong to the faint-hearted; it belongs to the brave."

The chief of state expresses American values. Presents awards. Welcomes visitors to the White House. The chief of state holds us up.

[WORLD'S TOUGHEST JOB]

Being president of the United States is a big job. There are many roles. Chief executive. Chief of state. Chief administrator. Chief **diplomat**. Commander in chief. Chief legislator. Chief of party. Plus the chief citizen.

The president represents the people. As commander in chief, the president runs the world's greatest army. The president decides what problems need fixing. As chief executive, the president manages the government. The government is like a big company. There are many different departments.

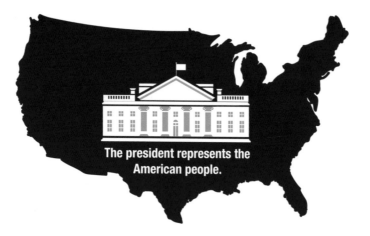

The president represents the American people.

It's the president's duty to help people and keep them safe. The president makes hard decisions each day. It's an around-the-clock job. The president's decisions can change the nation. "A president's hardest task is not to do what is right, but to know what is right," President Lyndon Johnson once said.

[SAY NO TO TYRANTS]

It wasn't always this way. Early American presidents didn't have much power. The Constitution was written that way. That's what the framers wanted. They created three branches of government. Each had a special job. Congress would make laws. Judges would interpret them. The president would carry them out.

The framers didn't trust executive power. Who could blame them? The U.S. had just won a war with England. King George III had too much power. He forced Americans to do things they did not want to do. The war

King George III

was over. The U.S. won. The old government was gone. A new one was made.

Event: Naming the First Chief Executive

Where: New York City

When: 1789

George Washington was the first U.S. president. What should people call him? That was what they asked. They thought long and hard. John Adams wanted to call Washington "Your Highness." It sparked a big fight in Congress. Others had names of their own. "His Exalted Highness." "His Elective Highness." "His Majesty the President."

"Why not call him George IV?" one senator asked. He was joking. Washington was not a king. Kings inherit their jobs. They rule for life. U.S. presidents are elected. They only serve for four years.

Washington was not an emperor. Emperors have absolute power. Just like kings. Presidents have limited power.

Senators fought. They finally came up with an answer. A simple name. "Mr. President."

Americans did not want the president to become a tyrant. They didn't want another king. So they gave the president only a few powers. Enforce laws. Veto them. Appoint judges and ambassadors. Run the military. Pardon criminals. Make treaties. But they didn't know how a president would do these things. One of the president's jobs was to receive officials from other nations. The president also had to give Congress a yearly update on the state of the nation. Today the speech is called the State of the Union.

[OFFICE CLERKS]

George Washington did it. So did some other early presidents. They stretched their power. Thomas Jefferson bought the Louisiana Territory. He didn't ask Congress for its okay. He just did it. America doubled in size overnight.

Abraham Lincoln was president during the Civil War. He took control of the government. He freed the slaves. Many called him a tyrant. A **dictator**. They thought he abused his power.

A few presidents were more like office clerks. They signed papers. Those presidents gave people jobs. They did not try to solve problems. James Buchanan was president before Lincoln. He didn't do much

James Buchanan

to stop the coming Civil War. Most presidents didn't work a full day. They took summers off.

Early presidents didn't even campaign to be elected. Others did that for them. Thomas Jefferson ran against John Adams. Insulting things were said. Bad names were used. One said Jefferson was "a mean-spirited, low-lived fellow." Jefferson's people said Adams was "one of the most **egregious** fools upon the continent."

[POWER PLAY]

Things slowly changed. Presidents gained more power from Congress. It was the early 1900s. The president was now the most important person in the government. Theodore Roosevelt. Woodrow Wilson. Both had great power. Especially when it came to dealing with other nations. They then left office. Three presidents followed them. They became clerks again.

Then came President Franklin D. Roosevelt. It was during the Great Depression. The **economy** failed. It was a terrible time in the U.S. Millions lost their homes. Jobs. Shops.

Roosevelt changed the role of the president. He played an active part in people's lives. Roosevelt started work programs. Saved banks and farms. He helped homeowners. Factory workers. Writers. Artists.

World War II (1939–1945) came. Roosevelt became even more powerful. He was popular. The president led the nation to victory. He died in office. The power of the president was great. Future presidents did not want to give that up.

There have been 44 administrations. But only 43 people have been president so far. Grover Cleveland served two **nonconsecutive** terms. He was president number 22 and 24. John Adams was number two. He knew how hard the job could be. "No man who ever held the office of president would congratulate a friend on obtaining it," he said.

FACES IN THE CROWD

George Washington
Born: February 22, 1732
Died: December 14, 1799

George Washington could have been president for a long time. There were no rules saying how long he could serve. Washington left after two terms. Each was four years. He set the example. Other presidents followed. Except Franklin D. Roosevelt. He was elected four times.

A law was written after Roosevelt died. Many Americans thought it was a bad idea for a president to serve more than eight years. They wanted to change the Constitution. In 1951, they did. The nation passed the 22nd Amendment. It stopped presidents from serving more than two terms.

Chapter 2
HAIL TO THE CHIEF

"What are you guys doing in my yard?"

A big smile crossed President Obama's face. Girl Scouts were camping. They were on the White House lawn. The White House is where the U.S. president works and lives.

The girls saw him. They screamed with happiness. The Scouts did not know the president would stop by and say hello. Soon the president and First Lady sat beside a campfire. The fire wasn't real. It was made of battery-powered lights. Everyone sang songs. They told jokes.

The White House had never hosted a campout. The president stayed with the Scouts for a bit. Then he had to leave. The girls ran toward him. They crowded around him. Some laughed. They shook his hand. Some hugged him.

"I didn't know he was going to come out," said one girl. "I thought he was too busy with work."

The president *was* at work. Talking with the Scouts was part of his job. The president of the U.S. wears many hats.

[CHIEF OF STATE]

Obama met the Scouts. He was wearing his chief-of-state hat. As chief of state, the president goes to funerals. Gives soldiers medals. Welcomes visitors to the White House. Makes **patriotic** speeches. Honors a championship sports team.

George W. Bush was president in 2001. On September 11, terrorists flew two planes into the World Trade Center. Thousands died. Bush later visited New York as chief of state. He grabbed a bullhorn from a firefighter. He stood on  the wreckage. The president started talking. People yelled. Someone called, "We can't hear you."

Bush spoke louder. He united the American people. "I can hear you!" he said. "The rest of the world hears you! And the people who knocked these buildings down will hear all of us soon."

[CHIEF EXECUTIVE]

The president is the chief executive. The chief executive decides how laws are to be enforced.

Four million people work for the executive branch. Some are cabinet heads. They are in charge of 15 departments. One is the Department of Defense.

It runs the military. Another is the Department of Justice. It makes sure people follow laws. Each department keeps the government running. The chief executive is the boss.

The chief executive picks people. They help run the government. Like Janet Reno. President Bill Clinton picked her to be attorney general. She was the nation's top cop. She had thousands of people working under her. The Department of Justice was her responsibility.

[CHIEF DIPLOMAT]

The president is also the nation's top diplomat. That means the president works with other countries. Negotiates treaties. Travels to see world leaders. The president talks to them. Tries to help them. The president also seeks

United Nations

their help. Such as taking action against terrorists.

President Obama once ran a
United Nations Security Council
meeting. It was in 2009. He was
acting as chief diplomat. The
United Nations is made up of
many countries. They try to solve world problems.

The president ran the meeting again. It was 2014. He called on nations to stop terrorists from traveling to Iraq and Syria. Those are two war-torn countries in the Middle East. In Syria, people fought a violent civil war. Many terrorists came there from other countries. Terrorists in Iraq were killing people too.

[COMMANDER IN CHIEF]

The president is also in charge of the military. The president decides where troops will go and fight. He orders warships to travel to other countries. The president decides how weapons will be used.

Generals and admirals have to

listen to the president. That's the way the framers wanted it. They didn't want a general to lead the government. They feared it might lead to **tyranny**.

Many presidents have served in the military. George Washington and Andrew Jackson both in the Revolutionary War. Zachary Taylor in the Mexican-American War. Ulysses S. Grant was a general. He led the Union in the Civil War. Theodore Roosevelt was in the cavalry. He fought in the Spanish-American War. Dwight D. Eisenhower, John F. Kennedy, and George H. W. Bush fought in World War II.

[LEADER OF THE PARTY]
A president is also the leader of their party. Political

parties are groups of people. They have the same ideas. The party members work together to win elections. The president helps people get elected. How? By giving speeches for them. And by asking for donations.

A president can run for reelection only once. Some have taken other government jobs when they leave office. William Howard Taft lost reelection. He became chief justice of the United States. Taft was the only person to ever have both jobs.

John Quincy Adams served one term as president. He lost the next election. Adams later won a seat in the House of Representatives. The former president became a powerful leader. He fought against slavery. Adams collapsed on the House floor in 1848. He died two days later.

[PROTECTOR OF THE ECONOMY]

The president takes credit when the economy is good. And when the economy is bad, the president takes the blame. Presidents spend a lot of time worrying about the economy. Most of the time it is out of their control. Things happen that can ruin the economy. Banks go broke. Prices go up. Unemployment rises. Things a president can't do much about. Yet a president is expected to keep the economy growing.

President Obama came into office in 2009. The economy was not good. Millions had lost their jobs.

They lost their homes. Things were a mess. The U.S. was in a **recession**. Obama met with his advisers. He met with Congress. They came up with a plan. The country spent billions on roads and bridges. The government gave money to banks. It didn't want them to fail. Carmakers were bailed out. Factories didn't have to close. The government did other things too. Slowly jobs returned. The economy got better.

ON THE JOB

Presidents can fire military generals. Harry S. Truman once fired General Douglas MacArthur. It was during the Korean War. MacArthur wanted to attack China. It was an ally of North Korea. Korea was split. The North was a U.S. enemy. Truman refused. He fired MacArthur.

→ HISTORY HAPPENED HERE

What: The Whiskey Rebellion

Where: Western Pennsylvania

When: 1794

A national liquor tax was passed in 1791. Congress ordered the tax. It needed to raise money. The tax had to be paid in cash. Many farmers couldn't pay. They didn't have money. Small farmers made whiskey. They used it to trade for things.

The farmers fought tax collectors. Resistance was strong in rural areas. Especially western Pennsylvania. President Washington spoke. He wouldn't let "a small portion of the United States dictate to the whole union."

The rebellion was a test for the new government. Could it make all citizens pay taxes? Would this law affect every state? The answer was yes. President Washington was the only sitting U.S. president to lead troops. He led almost 13,000 men. He arrived in Bedford, Pennsylvania. Then the president put General Henry Lee in charge. The rebellion soon fizzled. The power of the federal government was proven.

Chapter 3
ALL THE PRESIDENT'S STAFF

No one had ever been president before. What would a president do? George Washington thought about it. The Constitution gave the president power. He could veto laws. Appoint judges. Grant pardons. And the president was in charge of the military.

But Washington knew the president should be able to do more. The U.S. was a new country. It needed a strong person to guide it. The new president would have to keep the peace. He would have to hold the nation together. Washington didn't want to act like a king. That would be wrong. He hoped other presidents would follow his lead.

Washington did the only thing he could. He made it up as he went along. He slowly shaped the job. He created traditions. The new president did things the Constitution did not address. One tradition was to select a Supreme Court chief justice. The chief justice wasn't already on the court. That allowed future presidents to do the same.

President George Washington had worked on a treaty. Congress wanted to know about it. The president said no. He wanted to keep his papers secret. This is called executive **privilege**. Congress loved Washington. It didn't press him. But he did turn over some papers eventually. Presidents still use executive privilege.

Washington needed help. So he did something

presidents have been doing ever since. He picked a group of people to help him. They were his cabinet. The secretary of state was Thomas Jefferson. Alexander Hamilton was secretary of the treasury. The secretary of war was Henry Knox. And the attorney general was Edmund Randolph.

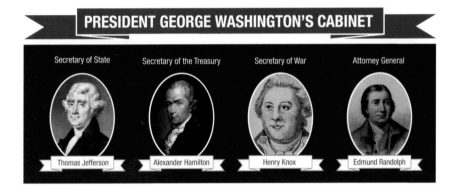

President Washington decided how the men worked with him. Their job was to **advise** him. To give him ideas. They helped him run the country. He also had an office staff. He picked three secretaries. One was his wife's nephew.

The term *cabinet* is not mentioned in the

Constitution. The men were appointed. James Madison made a note. He described them as "the president's cabinet." Presidents have been appointing cabinet heads ever since.

Think About It: *Are there too many departments for the chief executive to manage?*

[EXECUTIVE OFFICE OF THE PRESIDENT]

Oh, how things have changed. The president still needs advisers. There are many. Some are in the cabinet. Others work in different departments. More are on committees. The Council of Economic Advisers is one. Some advisers are on panels. One studies cancer. It is a disease. About 1,800 people work in the White House. They work for the president. Their office is called the EOP. The Executive Office of the President.

The White House chief of staff oversees the EOP. Congress approves some EOP workers. But most are hired directly by the president. The White House Communications Office is part of the EOP. So is the press secretary's office. The National Security Council is too.

The EOP does many things. It maintains the White House. The White House is the president's home. It's also a national historic symbol. It requires upkeep. The EOP's budget is nearly $700 million a year. The money is used to pay people and study problems.

It was 1939. Franklin D. Roosevelt created the EOP. He wanted to run things from the White

House. He brought in friends and advisers. They helped guide the nation. The EOP has grown over time.

The EOP has many offices. Each has a clear duty. Here are some of them.

Council of Economic Advisers: gives advice about the economy

Office of Public Engagement: makes it possible for people to talk to the president about issues important to them

Council on Environmental Quality: advises the president on environmental issues

Office of Science and Technology Policy: gives the president information on science and technology issues

[CHIEF OF STAFF]

The president's chief of staff runs the EOP. The chief of staff hires people. Fires them. Gives the president advice. Talks with Congress. The chief of staff puts the president's plans into action. And turns ideas into reality. This person is the president's most important employee.

"He is the one person besides the president's wife who can look him right in the eye and say, 'no, you cannot go down that road, trust me, it's a mistake,'" said Donald Rumsfeld. He was chief of staff to President Gerald Ford.

Is the chief of staff powerful? More powerful than the vice president? Many believe this is true.

[HEARTBEAT AWAY]

It was 1920. World War I was over. Republicans picked Warren G. Harding. He would run for president. They also picked Calvin Coolidge. He would run for vice president. Coolidge would be Harding's running mate.

Warren G. Harding and Calvin Coolidge

Coolidge's wife, Grace, was sad. She knew her husband wanted to be the president. He didn't want to be second.

"You're not going to take it, are you?" Grace asked.
"I suppose I'll have to," Coolidge said.

Harding won the election. He died three years later. Vice President Coolidge became President Coolidge. Grace became First Lady.

The story shows the **irony** of being vice president. It is the second highest office in the land. Yet the vice president has no real power. But all it takes is a heartbeat. And the vice president can become the most powerful person in the world.

"I am vice president," said Washington's vice president, John Adams. "In this I am nothing, but I may be everything."

[TWO JOBS]

The Constitution gives the vice president only two jobs. One is to take over if the sitting president dies, resigns, or is very sick. The vice president is

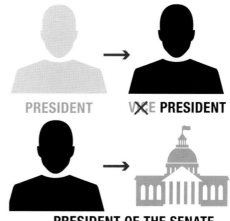

PRESIDENT   VICE PRESIDENT

PRESIDENT OF THE SENATE

also president of the Senate. If there is a tie, the vice president can break it. For decades, many ignored vice presidents. No one asked their opinion. Presidents rarely wanted their advice.

Harry S. Truman was Franklin D. Roosevelt's vice president. It was during World War II. They didn't talk much. Roosevelt never told Truman about the atomic bomb. Roosevelt died in office. Truman took over. Only then did he learn about the terrible weapon.

Presidents in recent years have come to rely more on the vice president. Al Gore helped Bill Clinton. Gore studied how to make government work better. George W. Bush depended on Dick Cheney. Cheney advised

Bill Clinton and Al Gore

him on national security. President Obama often asked Joe Biden's opinion. He wanted to know about foreign affairs. He asked about working with the Senate.

FACES IN THE CROWD

Eleanor Roosevelt
Born: October 11, 1884
Died: November 7, 1962

Edith Wilson
Born: October 15, 1872
Died: December 28, 1961

First Ladies can have power. Eleanor Roosevelt was very forceful. She was the wife of Franklin D. Roosevelt. He had a disease called polio. It is a virus. The president couldn't walk. Traveling was hard for him. Eleanor made the trips instead. She visited the poor and sick. Comforted people who were out of work. She told her husband what she saw. She reported what people said. People called her the "president's eyes, ears, and legs."

Edith Wilson was Woodrow Wilson's wife. He had a stroke while in office. The president was always in bed. He couldn't speak. Edith kept people from finding out. She lied to Congress and the public. She decided who could see him. The First Lady made sure he signed important papers. She even forced one cabinet member to quit his job.

Chapter 4
THE CABINET

Would Abraham Lincoln become president? He was not well known. Other men were more familiar. But he seemed the best choice. The most likely to win the North. The person who would save the Union.

Lincoln beat the others. He was on the **ballot**. Then he won the election. It was 1860. He was the first Republican president. Lincoln took office. Then he did something different. The president hired his political enemies.

The men didn't make it easy for Lincoln. Each had a strong will. All were better educated than their boss. Each thought he was smarter. Most were jealous.

It was a good move. Lincoln needed all the help he could get. His election split the U.S. The Southern states left the Union. They were afraid. Would Lincoln do away with slavery? Slavery was important to the South's economy. The South formed its own government. It was called the Confederacy.

Lincoln swore to keep the country together. But nothing could stop the Civil War.

Think About It: *Was Lincoln's idea to hire his enemies a good move?*

[LINCOLN'S TEAM]

It was 1860. Three other men wanted to be president. All were Republicans. Lincoln won. President Lincoln hired them. William H. Seward. He was a New York senator. Salmon P. Chase. He was Ohio's governor. And Edward Bates. He was a Missouri lawmaker. Seward was Lincoln's secretary of state. Chase, secretary of the treasury. And Bates was attorney general.

William H. Seward

Salmon P. Chase

Lincoln's team gave good advice. The men helped. The Union won the war. Lincoln saw their talent, common sense, and intelligence. "We needed to hold our own people together," he said. "These were the very strongest men. ... I had no right to deprive the country of their services."

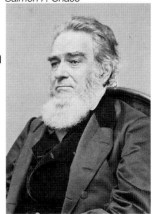
Edward Bates

HISTORY HAPPENED HERE

Event: Cabinet Meeting on the Emancipation Proclamation

Where: The Executive Mansion (Later Called the White House)

When: July 22, 1862

This was an important cabinet meeting. Lincoln wanted to free 3.5 million slaves. He wanted his cabinet's support. He wrote a paper. The Emancipation Proclamation. Lincoln read it aloud. It freed the slaves. But not in all slave states. Only in rebel states.

Each man listened. Some did not like it. Others did. William Seward spoke. He was secretary of state. Seward said to wait. The North needed a win. The Union was not doing well. They were losing battles. Seward felt the speech would be wrong.

"The wisdom of the view of the secretary of state struck me with very great force," Lincoln said. The president put the paper down. He did as Seward said. Lincoln waited for a Union win. It came two months later at Antietam. The slaves in rebel states were free.

[THE KITCHEN CABINET]

It was the beginning of Andrew Jackson's presidency. Cabinet members fought. The

Andrew Jackson

meetings upset the president. So he stopped them. He liked getting advice from his friends. This group was called the Kitchen Cabinet.

The president's friends were from Tennessee. Some were newspaper editors. The men were powerful and smart. They included Martin Van Buren. He was secretary of state. And John Eaton. He was secretary of war.

The term *kitchen cabinet* was meant to be rude. Today it is not negative.

[THE SATURDAY NIGHT MASSACRE]

On October 20, 1973, two key men quit. They worked for the president. The attorney general wouldn't fire the special prosecutor. The deputy attorney general also said no. Both quit their jobs. President Richard M. Nixon had ordered the firing.

A break-in was being investigated. The work was independent. The special prosecutor was hired. He looked at the facts. Were any laws broken? The prosecutor wanted White House tape recordings. Why? In 1972, five men were caught. They were inside Democratic Party offices. It was at the Watergate. That's in Washington, D.C. Recording devices were found. Bugs.

The president didn't order the break-in. But he found out. And a **cover-up** began. Maybe the tapes would prove it. President Nixon said no. He would not hand over the tapes.

It was a crisis. Never had a president attacked his own Justice Department. Nixon was helping himself. He was not protecting his office. His action angered the public. They turned against him. So did the press. The president's

Richard Nixon

rating fell. People disliked him. On August 9, 1974, Richard Nixon quit. He was the only U.S. president to do so.

[GROWING CABINET]

Every president has a cabinet. This is a group of advisers. They lead each department. Departments are part of the executive branch. Only four existed in Washington's day. Seven in Lincoln's.

EXECUTIVE DEPARTMENTS

Department of Agriculture (USDA)
Farming, agriculture, forestry, food

Department of Commerce (DOC)
Economic growth, jobs

Department of Defense (DOD)
National security, armed forces

Department of Education
Promotes student achievement

Department of Energy (DOE)
Nuclear energy, nuclear weapons, energy conservation

**Department of Health and
Human Services (HHS)**
Protects health, well-being

**Department of Homeland
Security (DHS)**
National security, natural disasters

Department of Housing and Urban Development (HUD)
Affordable homes, fair housing

Department of the Interior (DOI)
Federal land, natural resources

Department of Justice (DOJ)
Enforces and defends the law, public safety

Department of Labor (DOL)
Improves working conditions, promotes welfare of job seekers, wage earners, retirees

Department of State (DOS)
Foreign policy issues

Department of Transportation
Air, highway, rail safety

Department of the Treasury
Coins money, collects taxes, oversees banks

Department of Veterans Affairs (VA)
Supports military veterans

Today the cabinet has 16 people. This includes the vice president. There are 15 departments. Each has a leader. They are called secretaries. Except for the Department of Justice. The attorney general runs it.

Each department has workers. Four million in total. This includes the military. They keep the government running. Some collect money. Others write checks. Some take care of **veterans**. Still others protect the environment.

George Marshall
Born: December 31, 1880
Died: October 16, 1959

Harry Truman was president. George Marshall was secretary of state. After World War II, Europe was a wreck. Its economy was ruined. Many cities were destroyed. Communism was spreading. It was a different kind of government. Not a democracy. Americans were scared. They didn't like it.

Marshall came up with a plan. He hoped to stop communism. Western Europe would be rebuilt. It became known as the Marshall Plan. The U.S. spent $13 billion. It helped rebuild Europe. Communism didn't spread.

The president hires cabinet leaders. The Senate confirms them. Or rejects them. Presidents used to meet with their cabinets often. No longer. Cabinet meetings are not that regular. The White House staff has taken over most of the group's chores.

[WHO'S NEXT?]

The vice president's job is to become president. This is only if the president dies or cannot do the job. But what if the vice president dies? What if the

president dies too?
The government may
need other leaders.
Who would be next?
The vice president is
first, of course. The
Speaker of the House
of Representatives is
next. The president *pro*

tempore of the Senate is third. This person is a senator. And the senior member of the majority party. Cabinet members come next. There is an order. It is based on when each department was created.

PRESIDENTIAL LINE OF SUCCESSION

1. **Vice President**
2. **Speaker of the House**
3. **President Pro Tempore of the Senate**
4. **Secretary of State** (1789)
5. **Secretary of the Treasury** (1789)
6. **Secretary of Defense** (1789)
7. **Attorney General** (1789)
8. **Secretary of the Interior** (1849)
9. **Secretary of Agriculture** (1889)
10. **Secretary of Commerce** (1903)
11. **Secretary of Labor** (1913)
12. **Secretary of Health and Human Services** (1953)
13. **Secretary of Housing and Urban Development** (1965)
14. **Secretary of Transportation** (1966)
15. **Secretary of Energy** (1977)
16. **Secretary of Education** (1979)
17. **Secretary of Veterans Affairs** (1989)
18. **Secretary of Homeland Security** (2002)

Chapter 5
POWER CHECK

It was August 4, 1964. President Johnson had some news. He said the U.S. Navy had been attacked. North Vietnam had done it. It was wrong. Congress should approve hits back. The U.S. did not want a war. That's what Johnson said. Congress said okay. It agreed with Johnson. The U.S. fought back. But no war had been declared.

Only Congress can declare war. That's what the Constitution says. But Congress did not say okay to the Vietnam War.

It was November 1973. Congress passed the War Powers **Resolution**. It wanted more say. Troops should not be sent to fight. Not without approval.

The president must tell Congress about any use of force. The president has 48 hours to do so. What happens if Congress does not agree? The president must remove troops. Most presidents don't like the resolution. But all have followed it.

Think About It: *Does Congress do a good job of limiting the president's power?*

[THE CONSTITUTION SPEAKS]

The president's power goes up and down. The Constitution says what a president can do. Here is what's okay.

- Act as commander in chief
- Make treaties with other nations
- Veto bills
- Sign bills into law
- Appoint judges
- Pardon criminals
- Pick people to fill high-level jobs

Here is what's not okay.

- Make laws
- Declare war
- Borrow or spend money
- Raise taxes
- Do anything that robs citizens of "life, liberty, or property"

The Constitution also has built-in security. It's called checks and balances. They limit the powers of each branch of government. Each branch checks the power of the others. That way one branch does not dominate.

CHECKS AND BALANCES

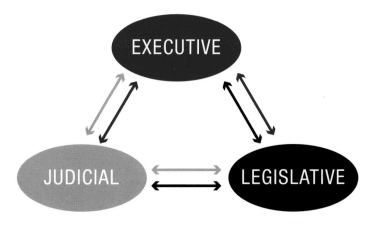

This limits what a president can do. It also gives the president power. Congress can make a law. A president can veto it. A court can convict criminals. A president can pardon them.

[EXECUTIVE ORDERS]

Presidents use executive orders. Orders tell federal workers to take action. The orders help the president run the executive branch. They do not require congressional approval. But they are laws. Presidents can avoid Congress.

Sometimes Congress doesn't say how a law should be carried out. It is up to the executive branch to make it happen.

Executive orders are legal. They are entered in the *Federal Register*. George Washington issued eight.

It was July 26, 1948. Harry Truman used an order. It was to **desegregate** the military. African American soldiers and white soldiers could serve in the same units.

Little Rock, Arkansas, in 1957. Nine African American students had tried to attend school. People blocked them. Spit at them. Called them names. The Arkansas National Guard also stopped them.

President Eisenhower used an executive order. It put the Guard under his control. The president sent the U.S. Army to Little Rock. Soldiers kept the peace at Central High School. It was an all-white school. All-white schools were illegal.

[UNPOPULAR]

Presidents can do many things. But sometimes they won't. They have to think about public opinion. A decision might be too unpopular. The people might not support it. The president might have to back down.

That happened to Franklin D. Roosevelt. The Supreme Court said some of his programs were illegal. The president was mad. He tried to change the court. "Reform" it. He wanted to appoint more justices. The president had to ask Congress. People got very mad. Congress said no. Roosevelt dropped his idea.

Health-care reform was a big topic. It was the early 1990s. The Clinton administration had a plan. But nobody could agree. Reform failed. Almost 20 years passed. It was a different story. The Affordable Care Act became law in 2010.

[EVOLUTION OF POWER]

The president's power has changed over the years. George Washington. John Adams. Thomas Jefferson. They shaped the office. The first presidents made it important.

ON THE JOB

There are three types of presidential actions. Executive orders. Presidential memoranda. And proclamations. View them all at *whitehouse.gov.* Memoranda can be very minor. They're not even counted in the *Federal Register*.

Andrew Jackson didn't like lawmakers. He vetoed many laws. More than the previous six presidents combined.

George Washington John Adams Thomas Jefferson James Madison James Monroe John Quincy Adams 1789–1829	VETOES 10	Andrew Jackson 1829–1837	VETOES 12

Abraham Lincoln had a war to fight. He didn't want Congress in the way. He stretched his power. Freeing the slaves was an executive order.

Theodore Roosevelt grew the president's power. So did Woodrow Wilson. Roosevelt expanded the nation's influence. He took the lead in foreign affairs.

Woodrow Wilson

Wilson helped write laws. He also influenced foreign relations.

Today's presidents can do many things. Congress can get angry. It gives the president a hard time. Once it took President Obama to court. The president gave an order on immigration. Congress said the order was illegal.

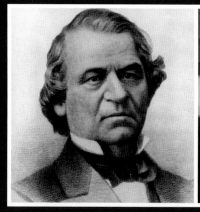

→ HISTORY HAPPENED HERE

Event: Impeaching the President

Who: Andrew Johnson and William Jefferson Clinton

When: 1868 and 1999

Presidents can be removed from office. But only if they do something wrong. It's the job of Congress to impeach them. Impeachment does not mean removal from office. It's a charge of misconduct.

It begins in the House of Representatives. House members vote on the charges. "High crimes and misdemeanors." The Senate then holds a trial. Two-thirds of its members must find the president guilty. What happens if the president is found guilty? The president must resign.

Only two presidents have been impeached. Johnson was the first. It happened in 1868. He disobeyed a law passed by Congress. Clinton was impeached in 1999. Congress charged him with lying in a court matter. They also charged him with trying to hide the crime.

Neither Johnson nor Clinton left office. The Senate never convicted them of any crime. Congress voted to remove Richard Nixon. But he quit before he was put on trial. He was the first president to resign.

Chapter 6
PUBLIC OPINION

President Obama had a lot to say. He gave a big speech. It's called the State of the Union. The president asked Congress to raise the national minimum wage. Congress was blocking the request. The president needed help. President Obama spoke to Congress. But he was really speaking to the American people. He wanted them to push Congress. Force it to raise wages.

"To everyone in this Congress who still refuses to raise the minimum wage, I say this: If you truly believe you could work full-time and support a family on less than $15,000 a year, go try it. If not, vote to give millions of the hardest-working people in America a raise."

Think About It: *Can the president change public opinion about a topic? How powerful is the art of persuasion?*

[A BIG STAGE]

The White House is a big stage. The president is the lead actor. The president talks. Millions listen. People are the most important part of government. People can make lawmakers do things. Things they might not want to do.

That's why presidents make speeches. Go on TV. Use social media. They try to get the people on their side. It's an old move. One called the "bully pulpit." In this case *bully* means to persuade. Theodore Roosevelt first used the

term. He was trying to get the people on his side. Roosevelt wanted people to live better. He wanted businesses to pay people more. Working conditions should be safer. The president gave speeches. He went from town to town.

Theodore Roosevelt

Roosevelt tried to unite the public.

"I suppose my critics will call that preaching, but I have got such a bully pulpit!" he said.

[CALL TO ACTION]

Presidents use the office for many reasons. They might want people to understand an issue. Educate them. The people can then push Congress to act. Perhaps to support a plan or a treaty. Presidents also use their power to blame Congress for blocking policies.

The president might also want people to do something. There was an energy crisis in the 1970s. The nation used  too much oil. Cars used too much gasoline. The U.S. depended on others for its oil supply. Gas prices went up. People waited in long lines. Some stations ran out of gas.

President Jimmy Carter went on TV. He talked to people. The president asked them not to use so much fuel. Reduce driving speeds. Turn down the heat in their homes. Some people did as he asked. Others did not. It was a good example of using the office to educate.

[THE GREAT COMMUNICATOR]

Can the president change opinions? Some say no. Ronald Reagan was called the "Great

Communicator." Reagan tried to create support for a rebel group in Nicaragua. That is a country in Central America. The rebels were fighting a leftist government. The public never supported his idea.

HISTORY HAPPENED HERE

Event: Senate Hearing on Capitol Hill

Who: Dee Snider, Frank Zappa, and John Denver

When: September 19, 1985

Musicians went to Capitol Hill in 1985. The Senate held a hearing on rock music lyrics. Parents Music Resource Center (PMRC) members wanted warning labels on records. The group started with Tipper Gore. She was the wife of then-senator Al Gore. Mrs. Gore had purchased Prince's *Purple Rain* album for her daughter. What she heard shocked her. She said she wouldn't have bought it had she known.

John Denver testified against censorship. So did Dee Snider of Twisted Sister. Frank Zappa said PMRC infringed on "the civil liberties of people who are not children."

U.S. record companies felt the pressure. They agreed to put warning stickers on their albums. Musicians were not happy.

Others say presidents can change opinions. But not like in the days of Theodore Roosevelt. Presidents talk about an issue. Frame it. Get people talking about it.

➤ HISTORY HAPPENED HERE

Who: President Jimmy Carter

What: Crisis of Confidence Speech

When: July 15, 1979

The energy crisis was in full swing. Few people thought President Jimmy Carter was doing a good job. He made many speeches about energy and conservation. People were not listening. He canceled a vacation. The president talked to many leaders. They blasted him. Polls showed people were upset. They no longer believed in America's future. Carter wrote another speech. Then he reached out.

He went on TV. Scolded people. He said people defined themselves "by what one owns." The speech ended. People agreed at first. They liked what Carter had to say. Then it backfired. It got ugly. People blamed Carter. They said the problems were his fault. It didn't help his reelection bid. He lost to Ronald Reagan in 1980.

Obama wanted more gun control laws. He made speeches. Tried to get people on his side. Many people supported him. But Congress did not.

[USING THE MEDIA]

Presidents don't just give speeches. They use media to get their point across. Media includes newspapers. Websites. Television. Magazines. Presidents talk to reporters. They appear on TV shows. Presidents even chat online. People can subscribe to the White House weekly podcast.

MEDIA & THE PRESIDENT

Media can change public opinion. Franklin D. Roosevelt was the first to use radio to talk directly to people. He eased their fears about war and the economy. The president talked about the state of the nation. These "fireside chats" were popular.

President Ronald Reagan was effective on TV. He could connect with people. Reagan and his advisers knew TV news was changing. Cable news was just beginning. The president appeared in many photographs. Reagan also made regular short speeches. The Reagan White House mastered the message.

Bill Clinton changed politics forever. He appeared on *The Arsenio Hall Show* in 1992. Clinton played the saxophone. He connected with Hall's young audience. Clinton was cool. The future president also appeared on MTV.

Social media has taken over. The president and his team tweet. The president tweets from @POTUS. President Obama has even posted selfies.

GLOSSARY

advise: suggest how something should be done

ballot: a list of candidates running for office; a ticket

cover-up: a plan to keep something secret or hidden from the public

desegregate: to make a place open to people of all races

dictator: the leader of a country who has total power

diplomat: a government employee who works with other countries and can create or maintain relationships with foreign leaders

economy: connected system of goods, services, and consumers in a country

egregious: bad; shocking

inauguration: to formally admit someone to office; a ceremony

irony: an outcome of an event other than what was expected; the difference between appearance and reality

nonconsecutive: not in order

patriotic: showing love and support for one's country

privilege: a special advantage or right that others do not have

race relations: relationships between people of different races in a community

recession: a time of economic difficulty, high unemployment, and negative growth

reform: to make changes in order to improve

resolution: a formal statement of an opinion or a decision given by an official group

roles: a part someone has in a situation; someone's function or purpose

tyranny: unjust, harsh, or cruel treatment by people with power

veterans: people who have served in the military

PRIMARY SOURCES
[A LOOK AT THE PAST]

What is a primary source? It is a document. Or a piece of art. Or an artifact. It was created in the past. A primary source can answer questions. It can also lead to more questions. Three primary sources are included in this book. **The Preamble to the U.S. Constitution**. It explains why the framers chose to create a republic. **The Bill of Rights**. It guarantees certain freedoms. And the **Declaration of Independence**. It stresses natural rights. More can be found at the National Archives (online at *archives.gov.*) These sources were written for the people. (That means us.) The people broke free from the king's tyranny. The United States of America was born. Read the primary sources. Be an eyewitness to history.

We the people of the United States, in order to form a more perfect Union, establish justice, insure domestic Tranquility, provide for the common defense, promote the general welfare, and secure the blessings of liberty to ourselves and our posterity, do ordain and establish this Constitution for the United States of America.

[PREAMBLE]

THE U.S. BILL OF RIGHTS

THE PREAMBLE TO THE BILL OF RIGHTS

CONGRESS OF THE UNITED STATES begun and held at the City of New York, Wednesday, March 4, 1789.

THE Conventions of a number of the states, having at the time of their adopting the Constitution, expressed a desire, in order to prevent misconstruction or abuse of its powers, that further declaratory and restrictive clauses should be added: And as extending the ground of public confidence in the government, will best ensure the beneficent ends of its institution.

RESOLVED by the Senate and House of Representatives of the United States of America, in Congress assembled, two-thirds of both Houses concurring, that the following Articles be proposed to the legislatures of the several states, as amendments to the Constitution of the United States, all, or any of which articles, when ratified by three-fourths of the said legislatures, to be valid to all intents and purposes, as part of the said Constitution; viz.

ARTICLES in addition to, and amendment of the Constitution of the United States of America, proposed by Congress, and ratified by the legislatures of the several states, pursuant to the fifth article of the original Constitution.

AMENDMENT I

Congress shall make no law respecting an establishment of religion, or prohibiting the free exercise thereof; or abridging the freedom of speech, or of the press; or the right of the people peaceably to assemble, and to petition the government for a redress of grievances.

AMENDMENT II

A well regulated militia, being necessary to the security of a free state, the right of the people to keep and bear arms, shall not be infringed.

AMENDMENT III

No soldier shall, in time of peace be quartered in any house, without the consent of the owner, nor in time of war, but in a manner to be prescribed by law.

AMENDMENT IV

The right of the people to be secure in their persons, houses, papers, and effects, against unreasonable searches and seizures, shall not be violated, and no warrants shall issue, but upon probable cause, supported by oath or affirmation, and particularly describing the place to be searched, and the persons or things to be seized.

AMENDMENT V

No person shall be held to answer for a capital, or otherwise infamous crime, unless on a presentment or indictment of a grand jury, except in cases arising in the land or naval forces, or in the militia, when in actual service in time of war or public danger; nor shall any person be subject for the same offense to be twice put in jeopardy of life or limb; nor shall be compelled in any criminal case to be a witness against himself, nor be deprived of life, liberty, or property, without due process of law; nor shall private property be taken for public use, without just compensation.

AMENDMENT VI

In all criminal prosecutions, the accused shall enjoy the right to a speedy and public trial, by an impartial jury of the state and district wherein the crime shall have been committed, which district shall have been previously ascertained by law, and to be informed of the nature and cause of the accusation; to be confronted with the witnesses against him; to have compulsory process for obtaining witnesses in his favor, and to have the assistance of counsel for his defense.

AMENDMENT VII

In suits at common law, where the value in controversy shall exceed 20 dollars, the right of trial by jury shall be preserved, and no fact tried by a jury, shall be otherwise re-examined in any court of the United States, than according to the rules of the common law.

AMENDMENT VIII

Excessive bail shall not be required, nor excessive fines imposed, nor cruel and unusual punishments inflicted.

AMENDMENT IX

The enumeration in the Constitution, of certain rights, shall not be construed to deny or disparage others retained by the people.

AMENDMENT X

The powers not delegated to the United States by the Constitution, nor prohibited by it to the states, are reserved to the states respectively, or to the people.

IN CONGRESS, JULY 4, 1776.

The unanimous Declaration of the thirteen United States of America,

When in the course of human events, it becomes necessary for one people to dissolve the political bands which have connected them with another, and to assume among the powers of the earth, the separate and equal station to which the laws of nature and of nature's god entitle them, a decent respect to the opinions of mankind requires that they should declare the causes which impel them to the separation.

ॐ⁓ॐ

We hold these truths to be self-evident, that all men are created equal, that they are endowed by their Creator with certain unalienable rights, that among these are life, liberty and the pursuit of happiness. That to secure these rights, governments are instituted among men, deriving their just powers from the consent of the governed. That whenever any form of government becomes destructive of these ends, it is the right of the people to alter or to abolish it, and to institute new government, laying its foundation on such principles and organizing its powers in such form, as to them shall seem most likely to effect their safety and happiness. Prudence, indeed, will dictate that governments long established should not be changed for light and transient causes; and accordingly all experience has shown, that mankind are more disposed to suffer, while evils are sufferable, than to right themselves by abolishing the forms to which they are accustomed. But when a long train of abuses and usurpations, pursuing invariably the same object evinces a design to reduce them under absolute despotism, it is their right, it is their duty, to throw off such government, and to provide new guards for their future security. Such has been the patient sufferance of these colonies; and such is now the necessity which constrains them to alter their former systems of government. The history of the present king of Great Britain is a history of repeated injuries and usurpations, all having in direct object the establishment of an absolute tyranny over these states. To prove this, let facts be submitted to a candid world.

He has refused his assent to laws, the most wholesome and necessary for the public good.

He has forbidden his governors to pass laws of immediate and pressing importance, unless suspended in their operation till his assent should be obtained; and when so suspended, he has utterly neglected to attend to them.

He has refused to pass other laws for the accommodation of large districts of people, unless those people would relinquish the right of representation in the legislature, a right inestimable to them and formidable to tyrants only.

He has called together legislative bodies at places unusual, uncomfortable, and distant from the depository of their public records, for the sole purpose of fatiguing them into compliance with his measures.

He has dissolved representative houses repeatedly, for opposing with manly firmness his invasions on the rights of the people.

He has refused for a long time, after such dissolutions, to cause others to be elected; whereby the legislative powers, incapable of annihilation, have returned to the people at large for their exercise; the state remaining in the mean time exposed to all the dangers of invasion from without, and convulsions within.

He has endeavored to prevent the population of these states; for that purpose obstructing the laws for naturalization of foreigners; refusing to pass others to encourage their migrations hither, and raising the conditions of new appropriations of lands.

He has obstructed the administration of justice, by refusing his assent to laws for establishing judiciary powers.

He has made judges dependent on his will alone, for the tenure of their offices, and the amount and payment of their salaries.

He has erected a multitude of new offices, and sent hither swarms of officers to harrass our people, and eat out their substance.

He has kept among us, in times of peace, standing armies without the consent of our legislatures.

He has affected to render the military independent of and superior to the civil power.

He has combined with others to subject us to a jurisdiction foreign to our constitution, and unacknowledged by our laws; giving his assent to their acts of pretended legislation:

For quartering large bodies of armed troops among us;

For protecting them, by a mock trial, from punishment for any murders which they should commit on the inhabitants of these states;

For cutting off our trade with all parts of the world;

For imposing taxes on us without our consent;

For depriving us in many cases, of the benefits of trial by jury;

For transporting us beyond seas to be tried for pretended offenses;

For abolishing the free system of English laws in a neighboring province, establishing therein an arbitrary government, and enlarging its boundaries so as to render it at once an example and fit instrument for introducing the same absolute rule into these colonies;

For taking away our charters, abolishing our most valuable laws, and altering fundamentally the forms of our governments;

For suspending our own legislatures, and declaring themselves invested with power to legislate for us in all cases whatsoever.

He has abdicated government here, by declaring us out of his protection and waging war against us.

He has plundered our seas, ravaged our coasts, burnt our towns, and destroyed the lives of our people.

He is at this time transporting large armies of foreign mercenaries to complete the works of death, desolation and tyranny, already begun with circumstances of cruelty and perfidy scarcely paralleled in the most barbarous ages, and totally unworthy the head of a civilized nation.

He has constrained our fellow citizens taken captive on the high seas to bear arms against their country, to become the executioners of their friends and brethren, or to fall themselves by their hands.

He has excited domestic insurrections amongst us, and has endeavored to bring on the inhabitants of our frontiers, the merciless Indian savages, whose known rule of warfare, is an undistinguished destruction of all ages, sexes and conditions.

[**DECLARATION OF INDEPENDENCE**]

In every stage of these oppressions we have petitioned for redress in the most humble terms: our repeated petitions have been answered only by repeated injury. A prince whose character is thus marked by every act which may define a tyrant, is unfit to be the ruler of a free people.

Nor have we been wanting in attentions to our Brittish brethren. We have warned them from time to time of attempts by their legislature to extend an unwarrantable jurisdiction over us. We have reminded them of the circumstances of our emigration and settlement here. We have appealed to their native justice and magnanimity, and we have conjured them by the ties of our common kindred to disavow these usurpations, which, would inevitably interrupt our connections and correspondence. They too have been deaf to the voice of justice and of consanguinity. We must, therefore, acquiesce in the necessity, which denounces our separation, and hold them, as we hold the rest of mankind, enemies in war, in peace friends.

We, therefore, the representatives of the United States of America, in General Congress, assembled, appealing to the Supreme Judge of the world for the rectitude of our intentions, do, in the name, and by authority of the good people of these colonies, solemnly publish and declare, that these united colonies are, and of right ought to be free and independent states; that they are absolved from all allegiance to the British Crown, and that all political connection between them and the state of Great Britain, is and ought to be totally dissolved; and that as free and independent states, they have full power to levy war, conclude peace, contract alliances, establish commerce, and to do all other acts and things which independent states may of right do. And for the support of this declaration, with a firm reliance on the protection of divine providence, we mutually pledge to each other our lives, our fortunes and our sacred honor.

There are 56 signatures on the Declaration. They appear in six columns.

COLUMN 1

GEORGIA

Button Gwinnett

Lyman Hall

George Walton

COLUMN 2

NORTH CAROLINA

William Hooper

Joseph Hewes

John Penn

SOUTH CAROLINA

Edward Rutledge

Thomas Heyward, Jr.

Thomas Lynch, Jr.

Arthur Middleton

COLUMN 3

MASSACHUSETTS

John Hancock

MARYLAND

Samuel Chase

William Paca

Thomas Stone

Charles Carroll of Carrollton

VIRGINIA

George Wythe

Richard Henry Lee

Thomas Jefferson

Benjamin Harrison

Thomas Nelson, Jr.

Francis Lightfoot Lee

Carter Braxton

COLUMN 4

PENNSYLVANIA

Robert Morris

Benjamin Rush

Benjamin Franklin

John Morton

George Clymer

James Smith

George Taylor

James Wilson

George Ross

DELAWARE

Caesar Rodney

George Read

Thomas McKean

COLUMN 5

NEW YORK

William Floyd

Philip Livingston

Francis Lewis

Lewis Morris

NEW JERSEY

Richard Stockton

John Witherspoon

Francis Hopkinson

John Hart

Abraham Clark

COLUMN 6

NEW HAMPSHIRE

Josiah Bartlett

William Whipple

MASSACHUSETTS

Samuel Adams

John Adams

Robert Treat Paine

Elbridge Gerry

RHODE ISLAND

Stephen Hopkins

William Ellery

CONNECTICUT

Roger Sherman

Samuel Huntington

William Williams

Oliver Wolcott

NEW HAMPSHIRE

Matthew Thornton

[DECLARATION OF INDEPENDENCE]

Be an engaged citizen in today's world.
Meet life's challenges after high school. Are
you fully prepared for democratic decision
making? Do you know how to address
and approach issues in a democratic
and responsible way? These five unique
handbooks will show you how.